MASTER, MISSION, MATE

MASTER, MISSION, MATE

A Guide for Christian Singles

KEN GRAVES

Published by Calvary Chapel Publishing (CCP)
A resource ministry of Calvary Chapel of Costa Mesa
3800 South Fairview Road
Santa Ana, CA 92704

First printing 2006
Printed in the United States of America
1 2 3 4 5 6 7 8 9 10 Printing/Year 10 09 08 07 06

Editor: Shannon Woodward
Cover Design: Aric Everson

Library of Congress Cataloging-in-Publication Data applied for

ISBN-10: 1-59751-021-1
ISBN-13: 978-1-59751-021-9

To my daughter, Jessica—
Who caused me to pray and think all these things through.
I am a father who is very grateful for the opportunity
to have raised so wise and strong a woman.
You are the greatest accomplishment of my life.

To my son, Micah—
A real man and an American hero.
I am proud of you.

To my wife, Jeanette—
Thank you for sticking around through all my learning.

To the Father of the fatherless,
Who has "counted" me faithful, putting me into His service.
Thanks Daddy.

CONTENTS

CONTENTS

ACKNOWLEDGMENT

I'm grateful to the men who have affected my life
with their teaching and preaching:
Fathers: Lawrence Esancy, Jim Summers,
Herbert Meppelink, Chuck Smith
Brothers: Bil Gallatin, Joe Focht, Bryon Burke

FOREWORD

It was winter in Maine when Calvary Chapel Bangor had their men's retreat. A few of the guys wanted to be baptized so their pastor Ken Graves cut a hole in the ice and jumped in. He was ready! When Ken came to our recent Men's Conference the place was packed and as he challenged the men, they roared their response. Ken has a voice from the wilderness, a fresh and unique, cutting-edge message that men, young and old, want to hear—Be God's Man!

It is my prayer when you read this guide that Jesus will be your *Master*, He will then determine your *Mission* in life, and He will direct you to the *Mate* who will help you to serve Him better.

Pastor Chuck Smith
Calvary Chapel Costa Mesa

CHAPTER 1

IT'S NOT YOUR IDEA

"behold, you are
fair, my love!"

song of solomon 1:15 (NKJV)

**THIS STUFF
DIDN'T
COME FROM
YOUR
HEAD.**

Have you read Song of Solomon lately?

I didn't think so. It's one of those books that frequently get overlooked. It's a book we don't often quote from, preach from, or read to our children. The passionate love being expressed here is sweet—but it just doesn't work well in public places.

The original language of Song of Solomon was Hebrew, of course, and it's a beautiful language, but whenever you go from one language to another, something gets lost in the translation. I'm convinced that these verses sound much prettier in Hebrew. Maybe it's just me, but every time I skim the pages and start reading those lines in English, I find myself hearing the words as if they were being read by someone with an inner city, New York accent.

Imagine that voice as you read the following verses from chapter four (I've changed the spelling just a bit to help you catch the accent): *"Behold thou art fair, my love; behold, thou art fair; thou hast doves' eyes widdin thy locks: thy hair is as a flocka goats, that appeah from Mount Gilead. Thy teeth are like a flocka sheep that are even shorn, which came up from the washing; whereof every one beah twins, and none is barren among 'em. Yeah. Thy lips are like a threada scahlet, and thy speech is comely: thy temples are like a piece of a . . . eh . . . pomegranate, yeah, that's it . . . pomegranate, widdin thy locks."*

Did you hear it?

Now, if you read that passage correctly—seriously, as I have not—you'll find that romantic love is God's idea. It's His invention. And all kidding aside, there's beauty here in the poetry and language of Song of Solomon. The beauty comes when you understand this book in its proper context. This is a passionate story, all right, but it's much bigger than just the account of Solomon and his Shulamite bride. This is the story of the passion between a different Groom and a different Bride—Christ and the church. Within those pages, you get to peek in on some sweet interaction between the Lord Jesus Christ and His Bride.

Does that surprise you? Have you considered that thought before—the idea that God not only created romantic love but also approves of it? It's true. Not only is God passionate in His love for you and for me, but He created romantic love for us to enjoy with our mate. You might *think* you're the inventor of romance, but you're not. This stuff didn't come from your head—it came from God's. The messed-up world we live in has taken God's invention and perverted it, but those of us who are called by His name have the capacity to fully experience the kind of romantic passion described in Song of Solomon. We can have that interaction with our spouse, and we can have that interaction with the Lord Jesus Himself.

Consider the heart behind these verses from Song of Solomon and elsewhere in the Scriptures:

> You have ravished my heart, my sister, my spouse; you have ravished my heart with one look of your eyes . . .
>
> Song of Solomon 4:9 (NKJV)

> All beautiful you are, my darling; there is no flaw in you.
>
> Song of Solomon 4:7 (NIV)

> The LORD has appeared of old to me, saying: "Yes, I have loved you with an everlasting love; Therefore with loving-kindness I have drawn you."
>
> Jeremiah 31:3 (NKJV)

> I will heal their backsliding, I will love them freely . . .
>
> Hosea 14:4

> As the bridegroom rejoiceth over the bride, so shall thy God rejoice over thee.
>
> Isaiah 62:5

> The LORD your God in your midst, The Mighty One, will save; He will rejoice over you with gladness, He will quiet you with His love, He will rejoice over you with singing.
>
> Zephaniah 3:17 (NKJV)

That's real love. That's a portrait of passion that differs greatly from the "love" the world croons about and swoons over—a love which lasts the length of a hit song or a popular movie, but which has very little staying power beyond that.

There's really only one reason why you're reading this book. It's because on some level, whether consciously or from a deep, subconscious desire, you want to find and experience that kind of passion—the love of two hearts joined together in God-ordained marriage. Before you can understand the right way to go about courtship and marriage, however, it helps to recognize the wrong way.

CHAPTER

2

THE WRONG WAY

"'for My thoughts
are not your thoughts,
nor are your ways My ways,'
says the LORD.
'for as the heavens
are higher than the earth,
so are My ways higher than your ways,
and My thoughts than your thoughts.'"

isaiah 55:8, 9 (NKJV)

You've been given the wrong message.

I don't have to know where you were born, where you grew up, who your parents are, or how long you've been a Christian—I can assure you that you've gathered a lot of false information as you've traveled through life.

Our culture bombards us with lies and empty promises. The world would have us believe that love comes and goes, that life is short and

THEY DON'T HAVE A CLUE.

you should do whatever you can to grab as much enjoyment out of it as possible, that you need to look out for yourself, and that the highest emotion you can feel is infatuation.

Consider, for a moment, all the movies you've watched, all the love songs you've heard, all the fiction books you've read. Woven into each of those is the not-so-subtle message that relationships are temporary, but you need-n't worry, because there's a better one waiting just around the corner.

Think about the artists who sing all those Top 40 love songs. Their messages sound pretty convincing within the confines of those three-and-a-half minutes, but take a longer look at their lives, and you'll see that they don't have a clue what real love is. The love they sing about is empty. Usually, by the time the song has hit it big on the charts, the person that artist is singing about isn't even in their life anymore—both parties have already moved on to the next relationship. For these peo-ple, relationships are only temporary. They're something you suck dry and then discard. These people—and the culture they represent—are in a vain and empty pursuit of some kind of fulfillment. Though they sound like experts, they really have no idea at all what they're singing about.

We live in this world, but we don't have to take our cues from it. In fact, we're told to resist the influence of the world. Romans 12:2, as paraphrased in the New Living Translation (NLT), says, *"Don't copy the behavior and customs of this world, but let God transform you into a new person by changing the way you think. Then you will know what God wants you to do, and you will know how good and pleasing and perfect his will really is."*

We're not to conform to what we hear and see. Instead, we're to *"be transformed by the renewing [of our minds],"* which happens only as you seek God and meditate on His Word. God's ways are different from the ways of the world. His ways are higher—and much, much better.

The world around us is in absolute rebellion against the Creator. As His children, we're called to live differently.

If we're to break the influence the world has over us, we have to first break our affection to this world. First John 2:15 warns us, saying, "*Love not the world, neither the things that are in the world. If any man love the world, the love of the Father is not in him.*"

Then it gives you a compelling reason for not following the ways of the world: "*For all that is in the world, the lust of the flesh, the lust of the eyes, and the pride of life, is not of the Father, but is of the world. And the world passeth away, and the lust thereof: but he that doeth the will of God abideth for ever*" (1 John 2:16–17).

The world's system is a temporary system—and one that is based on and driven by lust. The "*lust of the flesh*" is a lust for the 3 p's: *pleasure, power,* and *possessions.* That's what makes the world's system go round . . . and that's what causes so many problems for the world's inhabitants.

Most of us were indoctrinated into the world's system early. We got our first social experiences, our first social traumas, on the public school playground, where the rule of thumb is "dog eat dog." Out there, we battled for significance. We categorized each other, one-upped each other, and fought each other for positions of prominence. We put each other down to elevate ourselves, and stepped over and on top of anyone who stood in our way.

That's all you knew before you knew the Lord Jesus. Until you saw the alternative, until you realized the amazing fact that there's an entirely different kingdom existing side-by-side with the only one you ever knew, you didn't realize you had a choice. But now that you *do* belong to the Lord and you *are* a citizen of another kingdom, you need to set aside the old world system and learn how to follow the new.

The citizens of this new kingdom obey a different King than the one the world obeys. We follow the King who teaches that virtually everything in His kingdom is the opposite of the king-

WE LIVE IN THIS WORLD, BUT WE DON'T HAVE TO TAKE OUR **CUES FROM IT.**

dom we just escaped. Want to be great in this kingdom? You've got to get low. Aim for the bottom. Seek to be the servant to everyone. Want to get? You've got to give. Want to live? You've got to die.

These new rules are in complete opposition to the rules we used to follow—the rules the world still abides by.

Since we're new creations in Christ Jesus, we have to remember the calling placed on our lives. We've been called to leave the old and follow the new. That means you have to take an honest look at the way you approach situations and the thinking that leads you to action.

Just as it's wrong for you to date a series of people just to satisfy a taste for variety, it's also wrong for you to choose a mate and marry that person for selfish reasons. Let me offer a short list of inferior reasons—wrong reasons—to partner up with someone in marriage:

1. *It is wrong to marry someone just to make sex legal.* Some people do that. They know the seventh commandment tells them it's wrong to have sex outside marriage, so they figure the best way to keep from sinning is to make it legal. It's true that Paul said it's better to marry than to burn, but Paul was not endorsing sexual hunger as the primary motive for going out and finding a mate. That's a selfish—and wrong—reason to get married.

2. *It is wrong to marry someone just because they'll make you look good.* I'm not joking. You'd be surprised how many people have chosen mates simply for this reason alone. And you know what drives that motive? Pride. Plain, stinking pride. They find someone who has a look they like—a look that will reflect well upon them—and they go after the prize. Usually, such marriages don't last, and it's no surprise. When one partner makes a decision based solely on how it will benefit them, they're screaming out "It's all about me." Feeding your pride is a wrong motive for marriage.

3. *It is wrong to marry someone in order that you'll be served.* What, again, is the key to greatness in this new kingdom? It's getting low, taking the last place, learning to be the servant of all. So marrying someone just so you have a built-in servant is a lousy, selfish reason to marry. We're called to serve, not to be served. If we let our needs be met by Christ, we won't be so driven to latch onto our mate with a death-grip, demanding that they take care of us.

Our first thought, when seeking God's opinion on a potential mate, shouldn't be, "How well will this person serve me, Lord?" If you're in a relationship and you're scheming about how you can get that person to meet your needs, you still haven't got it. You don't yet understand exactly what you've been called to in this new kingdom. If that's the case, you need to spend some more time with the Lord Jesus and let Him undo the wrong thinking imprinted on you by the world.

But if you approach a potential mate with the thought of, "Is this the person, Lord Jesus, that You want me to partner up with? Is this someone I can serve on Your behalf—and someone who will join me in serving You?" then you've got it. Your perspective is right and good—and you fully understand the calling to lay your life down on behalf of another.

4. *It is wrong to marry someone just so you won't be alone.* We've all met people who fear solitude. "I just can't be alone!" they whimper. These people absolutely *must* be in a relationship. They go from one relationship to another to another. It's pathetic. And it's sad, because they're driven by their own perceived needs. I say "perceived" because the truth is, that's not a valid need. When you draw close to the Lord Jesus and you understand the depth of His love for you and you realize His eyes never leave you and there's never been a single step in life that you took alone, you understand that your dependency must be on Him alone. If you don't reach that place of Christ-dependence, you'll become an emotional black hole that will suck the life out of whoever comes too close to you.

So there's a list of wrong reasons for seeking and securing a mate. Each of those wrong reasons is motivated by a wrong kind of love—self-love. Real love, however, is not driven by lust, pride, selfishness, or need. Real love—God-fueled, God-glorifying love—can be summed up in this list from 1 Corinthians 13 (NKJV):

Love suffers long and is kind;
love does not envy;
love does not parade itself,
is not puffed up;
does not behave rudely,
does not seek its own,
is not provoked,
thinks no evil;
does not rejoice in iniquity, but rejoices in the truth;
bears all things,
believes all things,
hopes all things,
endures all things.
Love never fails.

Is it possible to love someone that purely? Are there right reasons to seek a mate? Is there a right way to go about finding that person?

Yes.

3

THE RIGHT WAY

"'for I know the thoughts that I think
toward you,' says the LORD,
'thoughts of peace and not of evil,
to give you a future and a hope.'"

jeremiah 29:11 (NKJV)

I'm guessing that you began your relationship with God early—before twenty, at least. I assume that because whenever I pose that ques-

THERE'S A PLAN FOR YOUR LIFE.

tion to large groups of people, I find that the vast majority came to some original relationship with the Lord Jesus while they were young. And that's a benefit. It's helpful. Because the younger you are when you first meet God, the less inclined you are to believe that the things that happen to you in your life are random occurrences.

But some still believe that. Some believe that they can walk aimlessly through life without following any sort of planned outline. That's just wrong. If you're a Christian, then there's a detailed plan already established for your life. All of it. Every part—including the choosing of your mate. Our Lord has established an order for how things are to happen, and even if most of the world thinks otherwise, it's important that you know the truth—and follow that outline.

Ideally, here's how it should work. You come to God. You make Him your Lord and your King—your Master. You accept the invitation to take up your cross and follow Him. And the longer you walk behind Him and with Him, the more you begin to understand how He views you, how He feels about you.

If the Lord Jesus Christ is your Master, then He will determine your mission. At some point, as you draw closer to Him, He begins to reveal to you the plan He's laid out for your life. Part of that mission includes being conformed into His image, into His likeness, but there's another part that is unique to you. The Lord will direct you to that thing you're intended to do with your life. He'll open your eyes to the things you've been gifted to do and help you navigate the choices you'll make about your occupation and how you might serve Him vocationally.

Then—and only then—should you begin to seek a mate who can help you fulfill that purpose. It's vital that you have some understanding of who you are before you go out looking for someone to match up with you. If you don't know who you are, you're not going to have any clue who you're looking for, or at least who you're hoping for.

That's not so hard, is it? But few people set about purposely to follow that outline. Instead, most people let lust, pride, or loneliness ignite their search for a mate—and they set out on that course with no thought at all to God, to their unique purpose in life, or to how a mate might fit in with their mission. Most people don't even understand they've been created for a mission.

Instead of following the world's routine, make it your goal, your ambition, to seek out God's plan. If you're reading this book, I expect that you already have some sort of relationship with the Lord Jesus. Maybe it's a new relationship, but it's there, nonetheless. I want that to strengthen. I want you to know Him so intimately that you easily hear His voice when He directs you to your mission. And then my prayer for you is that you rest in the knowledge that the Lord has a mate in mind for you and will direct you to that one person who can help you serve Him better, help you fulfill that mission He's set aside for you.

In the next three chapters, we're going to isolate each of those elements and talk about what each looks like in your life.

Master, Mission, Mate: the right way, in the right order.

CHAPTER

4

MASTER

"behold what manner of love
the Father has bestowed on us,
that we should be called
children of God!"

1 john 3:1 (NKJV)

MAYBE YOU'RE UNAWARE OF HOW GOD FEELS ABOUT ➡YOU.

Before you can consider the possibility of partnering up with someone for life, before you can begin the process of trying to choose someone out of this world of people, before we can even start a discussion on that whole subject, you have to begin with who you are. If you are a Christian, you are a child of the King. You're a member of a kingdom—a kingdom which, like its King, is not of this world. It's important that you understand that fact. It means that you, as a Christian, are an alien. This is not your home. Your home is elsewhere. As a Christian, you don't do things the same way everybody else does things here on earth. You're different.

One of the differences between you and a non-Christian is that you have a greater capacity to enjoy every good thing that God created. Why? Because you know the Maker. And you know—or you *should* know—that He created those good things with you in mind.

Right there, though, we hit on a possible conflict. Maybe you *don't* yet know that. Maybe you're unaware of how God feels about you, or how often He thinks about you, or how involved He is in the day-to-day happenings of your life.

It's hard to walk through this life without picking up some wrong thinking along the way. If you're to trust the God of the Universe with your life and your future—including your future mate—you have to chase out the wrong thinking and put some right thinking in its place.

Let's look at a quick list of lies. These are subtle but dangerous beliefs that creep into our thinking and affect our actions.

Lie #1: **God isn't aware.** If Satan can't get us to believe God isn't there, he'll get us to believe that God is there . . . but He's not aware. Many people have embraced this lie. "God spun the world into existence," they claim, "and then went off to start some other project on the other side of the galaxy. We're on our own down here."

Not true. Ours is not a "hands-off" Creator, but a God who closely monitors the smallest details in the lives of His created beings. *"But the very hairs of your head are all numbered"* (Matthew 10:30).

Lie #2: **God doesn't care.** This lie implies that God is there, and God is aware, but God just doesn't much care what you do with your life. He sees, but it doesn't matter to Him. He's disinterested, detached, and bored with humanity. The thinking that goes along with this lie is "One choice in life is as good as the next, as far as God's concerned. As long as I pick a path and follow it sincerely, I'm good to go."

Wrong. God has a will, an opinion, and a plan. You fit into that plan. Choices matter if you want your life to be blessed and if you want your life to count. *"Don't copy the behavior and customs of this world, but let God transform you into a new person by changing the way you think. Then you will know what God wants you to do, and you will know how good and pleasing and perfect his will really is"* (Romans 12:2 NLT).

Lie #3: **God loves me; God loves me not.** People fall into a fearful, paralyzing cycle of paranoia. They think, "When I'm good, I'm loved. But when I'm bad, I fall to the bottom of God's 'love list.' I'm ignored. He stops caring what I do and turns His attention to somebody higher up on the list."

Completely, utterly false. This reasoning gives us far too much responsibility. Think about it: you didn't create yourself. You don't keep your heart beating. Why then do you think you're responsible for keeping the love relationship between you and God going? His shoulders are much bigger than yours. He's much more capable, and far more faithful. *"If we are faithless, he will remain faithful . . ."* (2 Timothy 2:13 NIV).

That kind of thinking inflates our own sense of power and deflates God's. Those who buy into that lie usually embrace this one as well:

Lie #4: **God is smaller than my problems.** "God is there, He sees, He cares . . . but He's impotent. He just doesn't have what it's going to take to turn my life around, to set me on the right path, to bring me the right mate. I'll have to handle those details myself." Maybe no one actually says those words with their lips, but they shout them out by their actions. What else are you saying when you try to take the wheel yourself? What other message are you sending to God when you leave Him out of your major life decisions?

It's ridiculous to distrust God's power. The One who formed mountains and oceans and the solar system can certainly sort out whatever problems you think you have. *"Brace yourself, because I have some questions for you, and you must answer them. Where were you when I*

*laid the foundations of the earth? Tell me, if you know so much . . . .
Who defined the boundaries of the sea as it burst from the womb, and
as I clothed it with clouds and thick darkness? For I locked it behind
barred gates, limiting its shores. I said, 'Thus far and no farther will you*

HE'S NOT AN ABSENT, DETACHED, FICKLE, WEAK OR CRUEL GOD.

*come. Here your proud waves
must stop!' Have you ever com-
manded the morning to appear
and caused the dawn to rise in
the east? Have you ever told
the daylight to spread to the*

ends of the earth, to bring an end to the night's wickedness?" (Job
38:3,4; 8–13 NLT).

Lie #5: **God wants to squash my joy.** This lie is based on a picture of God as being some sort of old, brittle, sour meanie, who sits on
the edge of His throne with a giant hammer in hand, waiting to catch
you having some sort of fun. Those who believe this also believe that
nothing brings God more delight than when He manages to catch you,
spank you, and cage you.

Nothing could be further from the truth. The Lord Jesus had you in
mind when He made the sun and the moon and when He flung the stars
in the sky. He knew you'd look up now and then, and He wanted to
delight you. He was thinking of you when He created those things. He
was thinking of you when He invented love, passion, and romance too.
And why would He have created those things if He didn't want you to
enjoy life? *"The thief cometh not, but for to steal, and to kill, and to
destroy: I am come that they might have life, and that they might have it
more abundantly"* (John 10:10).

When you toss aside all the lies and look fully on the true God, the God who is good and great and kind, everything in life changes. Your capacity to enjoy those things God created for you grows large, as does your capacity to find happiness and fulfillment, because you have a relationship with the Maker, and you know that all those good things are expressions of His love for you.

He is not an absent, detached, fickle, weak, or cruel God. He's a God so full of love for you that:

He put that love in action by leaving heaven to come walk beside you (John 1:14).

He endured every temptation so He could sympathize with you (Hebrews 4:15).

He went to the cross so you could be His (Hebrews 12:2).

He chose you and loved you while you were in love with your sin (Romans 5:8).

He initiated your relationship and gave you the ability to love Him back (1 John 4:19).

He refuses to let anything come between you and Him (Romans 8:38–39).

Now, knowing all that . . . don't you want to serve Him?

CHAPTER **5**

MISSION

"for we are His workmanship,
created in Christ Jesus
for good works,
which God prepared beforehand
that we should walk in them."

ephesians 2:10 (NKJV)

When we talk about your mission, it's important you understand that we're really talking about two things. We're talking about *what* you do with your life and *why* you do it. I can't pinpoint for you exactly what your gifts are, exactly what plan the Lord Jesus has penned for your life. I can't determine your calling. For that, you're going to need to spend time on your knees seeking answers and direction from the One who made you and knows you intimately. But I *can* tell you how and why marriage fits into that plan.

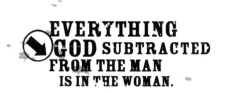

EVERYTHING GOD SUBTRACTED FROM THE MAN IS IN THE WOMAN.

First, though, a little background. I want us to go back to the garden, back to the place where it all started. There, in Eden, our Creator took a handful of dust, breathed into it, and brought to life the first man, Adam—a being who was made in the image of God.

When you consider God's acts of creation, you see that they were progressive in nature: God first spoke, and matter came into being. He then set matter into order, dividing light from darkness, water from land,

and so on. Creation became progressively better, progressively more complex. He then created the animals, and after the animals, He breathed life into Adam. To prove that Adam was set apart from the animals, to prove that he had been uniquely created with qualities not shared by those material creatures, God then brought the animals to Adam to be named. In so doing, God set Adam apart as superior to the rest of creation, showing that he alone was both spirit and matter. And for a time, Adam contented himself with this task.

But then God took creation to its ultimate culmination. In an acknowledgment that animal companionship was not enough for Adam—that Adam was lonely and in need of a partner—God caused him to fall into a deep sleep and divided him into two beings.

To understand the significance of this act, we have to consider what God did *not* do. What He did not do was to repeat the creative act He had performed in Adam. He did not reach down again into the dust and breathe life into a handful of inert matter. Instead, He took the man who bore His image and split those attributes into two separate but complementary beings. He did not make her separate from Adam but rather, He separated her out of Adam. God took more than just material, more than just bone, more than just a rib. The language actually indicates that God took one whole side from who Adam was and made another complete person. Adam was divided: body, soul, and spirit. And in this final act of creation, God further divided His image.

You see, there are two sides to our Creator's personality. We see this clearly in the Lord Jesus, the image of the invisible God, who, in His earthly life, demonstrated those two halves: lion and lamb. He could whip, and He could weep. Everything that we tend to relate to as being masculine and feminine is there, in our Father, and in His Son.

I believe those two halves were also in Adam, in his original state of being. I believe he bore the full image of God—fully lion, and fully lamb. When God took part of Adam to create Eve, He divided this image into the two beings, effectively isolating the lamb from the lion. Man naturally has more of the strength of the lion; woman naturally has more of the gentleness of the lamb. You may call this a generalization, but I maintain that it is still generally true.

Our rebellious culture has sought to undo what God did in Genesis chapter two. "Men should be more like women," they say, "and women should be more like men." Either they push the genders to emulate each other, or they blame male and female differences on media indoctrination. Egalitarianism tries to deny the beautiful differences between the sexes. At the same time, it attacks the very differences that it says don't exist—which is absurd. The pure truth of the matter is this: God divided His image into two beings that can come together through marriage and complete each other and become one.

Eve was given an interesting title in Genesis chapter two. Before she drew her first breath, her calling was identified. She was to be a helper to Adam. A helper for what? We have to address this question, because as I've traveled around the country speaking to groups of men, it's become obvious to me that most men do not understand why God made women. It's simple: men need help. Adam . . . his sons . . . men today . . . we've all needed help.

But what did God have in mind? Was Eve needed for tending paradise? Was she simply there as an assistant gardener? No. Adam didn't need a gardening partner. That's because Adam's chief purpose for living was not so that God would have a nice garden to visit in Eden. God made man to know and enjoy and worship his Maker—to have a relationship with Him. So when God declares that Adam needs Eve, He's speaking about this chief purpose. He's saying, "Adam, the romance that you and your wife will share will enable you to know and enjoy and love Me more fully." Eve was to help him in this, you see.

When Adam woke from that sleep, I believe he knew immediately that he was different. And it wasn't just the fact that he was missing some of his material, some of his bone and his flesh. He wasn't the same, and he knew it. Part of the image of his Creator had left him. He realized that he'd lost some of the capacity he'd had to feel things emotionally. He was a little less balanced, a little more aggressive—a lot less lamb, but with the same degree of lion.

My whole life I've heard—as I'm sure you have heard—the fairy tale that "every man must get in touch with his feminine side." Let me state clearly on behalf of the One who made us: Men, you do not have a feminine side! It was removed by God that day recorded in Genesis chapter two.

BY DESIGN, MEN & WOMEN ARE INDISPUTABLY DIFFERENT, BUT WE COME TOGETHER—IN GOD'S PLAN—AS A MATCHING SET.

The differences between the genders cannot be erased. Unless you've been in college too long, you're well aware of those differences. Men and women have totally different ways of looking at life. God created man for war, and every single boy ever reproduced came out that way—looking for a fight. Boys come out dreaming of overcoming and conquering. It's built into a man. And every time he looks at life, even little bits of life, he looks at it as something to overcome. There's something to fix, some challenge, something to tinker with. That's how God made us.

But God made women differently—He created them for relationship. He made them to be sympathizers, communicators. Little girls come out determined to learn to communicate as quickly as they can so they can have relationships. Boys make sound effects. Girls make relationships. If a young girl can't make a relationship, she'll buy herself one. "Hey, if you do this or that I'll be your best friend." Try that with a little boy and he'll say, "I don't need you as a best friend, I've got all kinds of friends."

By design, men and women are indisputably different, but we come together—in God's plan—as a matching set. Everything that God subtracted from the man is in the woman. When we understand that equation, criticism turns to appreciation. Instead of finding fault with our differences, we can enjoy them.

Worldwide right now, in our generation, there's a war raging against manhood. This rebellious world is fighting furiously to undo what God has done. Their efforts have brought nothing but confusion. Men have been emasculated, and it's no wonder that in this atmosphere of confusion and upheaval, men and women cannot fathom the mystery of "the two becoming one."

I dislike even mentioning homosexuality in this context, but I must, for it is relative. Despite what the world would have us all believe, two members of the same gender cannot ever become one in the way that God has designed—in a way that will bring the two halves of His image together again in holy matrimony. The image of the One who made us can only be fully reflected in a man-woman union, in marriage.

God gave us marriage for a reason. It was God Himself who looked at a single man—a perfect single man—and said, "This picture is not complete." When a man finds a woman to partner with for life, he finds a good thing. He finds someone who can help him in four ways:

She can help him draw closer to God and more fully understand what it is to love and be loved. In other words, she can provide for him a reference point that will help him to better understand the relationship God desires between Himself and His children.

She can assist him as he fulfills his calling in life, helping him to serve God better. If God brings you a mate, it's because there's work the two of you can do together better than you could do alone.

She can help him reproduce godly seed. We're called to not just reproduce ourselves physically on the earth, but spiritually as well. Our mandate to go and make disciples does not just apply to strangers.

God desires that we reproduce people of faith, starting right in our own homes.

She can give him spiritual reinforcement. Ecclesiastes 4:9–10 says this: "Two are better than one, because they have a good reward for their labor. For if they fall, one will lift up his companion" (NKJV).

How good it is to have a godly partner! And if two are better than one, imagine the increased benefit of having three in your marriage—you, your spouse, and the Lord Jesus. A marriage united in Christ is a marriage bound by a threefold cord. Ecclesiastes 4 goes on to say, in verse 12, "Though one may be overpowered by another, two can withstand him. And a threefold cord is not quickly broken" (NKJV).

When Jeanette and I were shopping for wedding rings, we looked for a Christian jeweler who would engrave the word _Jesus_ on our bands, because we understood, going in, that unless our union was a three-party deal, we'd be doomed from the start. As descendents of dysfunctional people, and sinners ourselves, we knew that without the help of our Lord—who would teach us, guide us, and show us how to reinforce one another spiritually—our marriage probably wouldn't survive.

In any discussion of marriage, at some point you have to address the question of celibacy—actually, the gift of celibacy. Now if, when I say "gift of celibacy," you automatically think, _Oh, I hope I don't have that gift_ . . . then I assure you, you don't. If it would not be a gift to you, then you don't have that gift. The calling is definitely out there. God does call some to that, although I believe it's comparatively rare. Proverbs 18:12 says that he who finds a wife finds a good thing and obtains the favor of the Lord. You should write that one down, maybe memorize it. He that finds a wife finds a good thing. God says it's good. It's a blessing. If you find a wife, you obtain the favor of the Lord.

Assuming your heart does not leap for joy at the thought of a celibate life, the next question arises: who am I looking for? Good question.

CHAPTER 6

MATE

"and Adam said, 'this is now bone
of my bones, and flesh of my flesh;
she shall be called Woman,
because she was taken out of Man.'
therefore shall a man leave
his father and his mother
and shall cleave unto his wife:
and they shall be one flesh."

genesis 2:23, 24

You know who you are and where you came from and who you belong to. You know how a mate will enable you to fulfill your particular mission in life. Now it's time to know who you're looking for.

Sounds simplistic, doesn't it? But it's too important not to spell out: you've got to know who it is you're looking for. You don't just go wandering out in the world waiting for someone to club you over the head. Or you don't just walk around waiting for someone to steal your attention and your affection away. Rather, you need to go out quite purposefully, knowing exactly what you're looking for.

Since you've spent time getting to know the Lord Jesus, your Master and your King, you need to now wait until you recognize Him in someone else. Men: you need a Jesus woman. Women: you need a Jesus man. It's that simple.

The Jesus man or the Jesus woman you're looking for won't have it all together, but they'll be in process. They may be imperfect, but they're under construction. They're being changed into the likeness of our Lord Jesus, as you are.

How will you be able to recognize that? Well, you have to first make sure you're growing in your own relationship with Christ. That's essential. So if you're a baby Christian, I highly recommend that you put all of this other stuff on hold. If your relationship with the Lord Jesus is that new, don't be in a hurry. Just slow down, mellow out, and give yourself time to grow in your relationship with Him.

I offer that warning because the truth is you can easily rush into a mistake and sign up for life with somebody and then be stuck. While you both should be learning to grow in your relationship with one another, you can't focus on that because you're too busy trying to learn how to have a relationship with God first. Do yourself a favor. Establish yourself with the Lord Jesus before you try to establish yourself with someone else.

Along those same lines, I have to warn you of another trap. Be careful that you don't latch onto someone just because he or she shows up at church. Remember something: the church is a hospital. That means there are a lot of sick people sitting on your right and left each week—people who are *not* ready to enter into a meaningful, life-committing relationship. Just because you meet someone at church doesn't mean he's Mr. Right or she's Miss Right. They could easily be Mr. or Miss Sick.

There are a couple of practical reasons why you need to marry a true believer, besides the obvious—which is that God forbade you from marrying an unbeliever. In 2 Corinthians 6:14 He says, "*Do not be yoked together with unbelievers. For what do righteousness and wickedness have in common? Or what fellowship can light have with darkness?'* (NIV).

You cannot fellowship with an unbeliever. You can be a friend with an unbeliever, yes. Adam could be a friend to the animals in the garden, too. But he couldn't fellowship with them. God didn't find a mate for Adam among the creatures in the garden, because it wasn't possible for Adam to have the intimate relationship he needed with a being that was unlike him. It is against God's design for two different kinds to come together and try to be one. In the same way, you cannot have intimate fellowship with an unbeliever, a heathen, because intimate fellowship is a connection of two spirits—and you cannot be one in spirit with someone who is spiritually dead.

So on the basis of obedience alone, you need to wait until you find a believer. And if you do, you'll be rewarded in two ways: you'll avoid misery, and you'll gain blessing.

The misery comes when you meet a person who is not yet a believer and you decide that missionary dating will fix that problem. It won't.

Men, God has not called you to go and find a woman and then win her to Christ after you marry her. Women, the same goes for you. Missionary dating is not an effective ministry. Very rarely—in total grace situations—a story such as that that turns out well. Somebody married an idiot and then he got saved. I've seen it happen, but it's extremely rare. I marvel every time I come upon a situation like that. But usually, on the way to that miracle, there's a great deal of suffering. There's so much suffering, in fact, that if you approach someone who tried to snag a mate this way and ask them if they recommend their approach, they'll tell you bluntly, "That's not the way to do it."

Take my advice—and the advice of anyone who tried missionary dating and suffered the consequences. Don't do it. Dating and/or marrying an unbeliever is not an option. Don't even bother praying about it.

This third warning seems like a no-brainer, but it must be said. Married people are also not an option. I don't care how perfect that man or woman is. I don't care how great you feel when you're around them or how certain you are that the power of your infatuation with one another will overcome the mess of a divorce. It won't. You don't find God's mate for you by breaking up a marriage. You know that, right?

So if you're not looking for a heathen or an already-married person, who exactly are you looking for? If you're a man, you're looking for the woman described in Proverbs 31. What a gal! What a lady! Women like this are quality women—full of virtue and character. I'm married to one of those women, so I can testify. Here's where the blessing comes in. If you do it God's way—which is to wait until a spiritually mature believer comes along—you'll be rewarded with a mate who really knows how to love and bless you the rest of your life. It's stated that way in Proverbs 31:12: "*She will do him good and not evil all the days of her life.*" That's the blessing you want. That's the reward worth waiting for. Don't be taken in by someone who's physically attractive but spiritually empty. Wait for your Proverbs 31 woman to come along.

DO YOURSELF A FAVOR. ESTABLISH YOURSELF WITH CHRIST BEFORE YOU TRY TO ESTABLISH YOURSELF WITH SOMEONE ELSE.

Women, you have a scriptural counterpart too. You're waiting for a 1 Timothy 3 man. You may not have ever considered that passage in the light of marriage before, but there's your list. All you single ladies, get to be experts of this third chapter of Timothy. That's who you need to be looking for. There you'll find all the character qualities of a man who the Lord Jesus wants running things in His church. It just so happens that those same qualities are needed for running a household, for heading a family. When you agree to marry a man, you're agreeing to submit to him. Don't you want to submit to a man with all those godly characteristics? If you're going to be asked to submit to somebody, you're better off submitting to somebody who is so mature, so godly, that he could be in leadership within the church, because when the two of you marry, your family is going to become a church. He's going to be the pastor. So choose well. Choose prayerfully.

When you look at the life of that Christian man that you're considering, look for some order. Ask yourself: does he manage what he's been given by the Lord right now? Does he manage his life well, or is it a wreck? Are you looking at a guy who's a slob? Oh, maybe his hygiene is fine, but you get in his truck and it's a personal trash-wagon. His financial affairs are a wreck. I mean, those kind of things are indicative of how this man's going to run your house, how he's going to manage your life together. (Note to the men: clean out your truck once in a while, okay?)

And finally, men and women, you're looking for someone you can bless. That may sound contrary to what I said above about the

Proverbs 31 woman—that if you wait for her, she'll bless you for as long as she lives. But the truth is, you have to give before you get.

Look at the example the Lord Jesus gave us. We love Him because He first loved us. And not only did He love us first, He loved us while we were yet sinners. It was then that He laid His life down for us. That example should be the reference point for those of you who are looking for a life partner. Who can I help? Who can I bless? Who can the Lord love through me? The beautiful surprise to all this is that when you give like that, you get. You receive back. When you approach marriage like the Ephesians 5 man, willing to lay down your life for your bride, as the Lord Jesus laid His down for the Church, your love will win her over—and she'll desire to bless you in return.

That's the real test of whether or not you're ready to get married: are you looking for someone to serve you, or someone you can serve?

One last time, here's your checklist. You're looking for a person who is:

- Already a believer in Christ—a Jesus man or woman
- Not already married
- Not focused on their own needs and desires, but rather, seeks to serve God

So now that you know who you're looking for, it's time to grab your binoculars, roll up your sleeves, and hit the pavement, right?

Wrong. Now it's time to take a nap.

CHAPTER **7**

TAKE A NAP

"and the LORD God caused a deep sleep
to fall upon Adam, and he slept . . ."

genesis 2:21

IF YOU **NEED** A MATE, **GOD** WILL BRING YOU A MATE.

It's tempting, when you've grasped this whole concept and you've gone through the list and you have a good understanding of who it is you're looking for, to start looking. It's tempting, but it's not necessary. You don't have to be out there working feverishly to find your life partner—because the Lord Jesus is already at work, already seeking. He's already involved in the quest.

You need to get a handle on that truth. Want a scriptural example? Let's look at Genesis 24.

Abraham, the Scripture tells us, was "*well advanced in age.*" He was getting old, and he wanted to find a bride for his son. So he tells his chief servant—the oldest servant of his household—to go and find a wife for Isaac. And he stipulates that this wife was not to be chosen from the Canaanites, with whom Abraham dwelt, but from among Abraham's own people.

Note in verse 5 that the servant asks Abraham if he should bring Isaac with him to Abraham's former homeland. It makes sense, right? After all, if this bride is to be for Isaac, wouldn't it stand to reason that Isaac would take part in the search? But what does Abraham say? "Do not take my son." Isaac is not to participate in this search. The bride would be brought to him.

Do you understand the promise implied in that passage? You're no different than Isaac. If you need a mate, God will bring you a mate. You cooperate in this search by not searching, but by resting and trusting.

It can be hard to trust. Your flesh will rebel against resting and cause you to think that maybe our Lord isn't aware of how much you need a mate, or that He's so busy running the universe, He hasn't noticed how alone you are. When those troubling thoughts come, pick up your Bible and go back to Genesis 2. Remember that it was God who was first aware of Adam's need, God who said, "*I will make him a helper.*" That should comfort you. If God saw Adam's need, He sees your need too.

What we don't read in that passage is that Adam initiated the hunt or did anything to try to fix the problem himself. He didn't even know there *was* a problem. In fact, all Adam did was sleep. He went into a deep sleep, and you know what? That's a great place to meet somebody—when you're not out conducting interviews, not out in pursuit, but rather, you're socially in a deep sleep. You're busy about your Father's business and you've just kind of gone to sleep on the matter.

Undoubtedly, there will be those who, when they read that, think, "That's easy for you to say! You're already married!" I've heard that a lot from the chronically single—those who don't want to be single and feel that enough time has gone by and they don't want someone advising them to "just go to sleep." But you have to remember the old adage: "A watched pot never boils." It's true. When you are the most anxious, things move the slowest, don't they? You can save yourself a lot of suffering and a lot of mental anguish, I believe, if you just get busy doing whatever the Lord Jesus has given you to do.

In the passage about Isaac, we need to understand that Abraham's chief servant was a type of the Holy Spirit. God worked through that chief servant to select a bride for Isaac. In the same way, God is at work in the Holy Spirit on your behalf as well. He's going through the selection process this moment. Our Lord cares. In fact, He cares more about this subject and is more in tune with your need for a life partner than you are. So when you feel tempted to check the pot again to see if it's boiling yet, don't. Resist that impulse. Instead, get busy doing kingdom work. Trust Him.

On that note, if you haven't already done so, memorize Proverbs 3:5 and 6. "*Trust in the L*ORD *with all your heart, and lean not on your own understanding; in all your ways acknowledge Him, and He shall direct your paths*" (NKJV).

He will direct your path. *He* will. It's not something you do for yourself. Bring your desire to the Lord Jesus, ask Him to have His perfect way with your life, and let it go. When we try to lean on our own understanding, we get ourselves in trouble. We can't know the secrets of what is in another person's heart, and we don't know the future. And it's a mistake to rely on the little bit we *do* know.

Trust Him implicitly. Let it go. And take a nap.

CHAPTER 8

GET A LEASH

"the heart is deceitful
above all things,
and desperately wicked;
who can know it?"

jeremiah 17:9

Oh, but the heart is wicked.

It can't be trusted. It absolutely shouldn't be depended on. And though you search the Scriptures diligently, you'll never find a single verse that encourages you to follow your heart. But you are told to *guard* your heart. Proverbs 4:23 gives us this sober warning: "*Above all else, guard your heart, for it is the wellspring of life*" (NIV). Other versions tell you to keep it or watch over it.

Why is it so important to keep a watchful eye on the heart? Jeremiah 17:9 gives us the answer: "*The heart is deceitful above all things, and desperately wicked; who can know it?*" Desperately wicked. Do you

want to follow something that is desperately wicked? Of course you don't.

If you were given a chance to partner up— let's say, go into business—with someone who was described to you as being deceitful above all other people and desperately wicked, would you do it? You wouldn't. You wouldn't want anything to do with that sort of person. You'd steer yourself clear of someone with a proven record of being unfaithful, unreliable, deceitful, and wicked. And yet—that's a description of your heart. Your heart is all those things. The heart of man is the most wicked, desperate, mischievous thing there is. Knowing that, you can understand why the Scriptures speak so negatively about the heart. You can better understand why Proverbs 28:26 says, "*He that trusteth in his own heart is a fool.*" You can't get much plainer than that. If you trust in your own heart, you're an idiot.

While you're waiting for the Lord Jesus to bring a mate to you, your job is to guard your heart. I urge you to commit to that. That's the single best way you can cooperate with God in the search for a life partner.

Throughout the book of Proverbs, you'll find a number of verses that tell you to put a leash on your heart, implying that you should actually take command and assume control over your heart. When the Lord Jesus gave the Sermon on the Mount, He taught a sure-fire method for controlling the heart. In Matthew 6:21, He explained that the heart goes after whatever it decides to treasure. "*For where your treasure is, there will your heart be also.*" Remember that?

I can't even tell you how many times people have come to me with some issue of the heart and complained that they couldn't control their emotions. "I can't help how I feel," they insist. Maybe you've heard that same complaint. Maybe you've uttered that same complaint. Well, the truth is that you *can* help how you feel. You can take control of your heart—and therefore, your emotions—and determine the direction your heart will go. What you have to do is get a leash and rein it in. When it tries to gallop off, you've got to deal with it firmly. "Whoa, now! You're not going in that direction . . . get back here!" You've got to yank that thing and make it go where you want it to go.

Colossians 3:2 tells us to "*Set your affection on things above, not on things on the earth.*" Remember those goofy Warner Bros. cartoons? Remember Wile Coyote and all those Acme products? In just about every episode, Wile Coyote would build some sort of heat-seeking missile meant to track down the Road Runner. You know what happened. He'd turn the dial and set it loose, and when it got close to the Road Runner, the bird would just hop on the missile, fiddle with the dial, and turn it loose again—to seek and destroy Wile Coyote. That mangy dog never did learn. In the same way, guys, there's a dial in your heart. In your heart and mine, there's a dial. And you are in control of where you set that thing. You can set it to seek the Lord Jesus or you can set it to seek the temporary, transitory things of this world.

I can't urge you strongly enough. Seek the Lord. Set your affections on things of God. Guard your heart and keep your emotions in check.

Now, I have a specific warning for all you single people. Actually, I say this to those of you who are married as well. *Romantic feelings can be very dangerous.* In the wrong context, romantic feelings can be deadly.

Fire can be a good thing, wouldn't you agree? It can also be a bad thing, but when it's used to a good purpose, it can be a beneficial tool. The last time you left your house, you most likely did so with the aid of fire. These little fires ignited under the hood of your car and each one of the pistons in your engine was harnessed to deliver you to your destination.

Fire in your furnace is a good thing because it enables you to warm your whole house. But if it gets out of that proper context, it can destroy you. A campfire can be a lifesaver, but a campfire that jumps its boundaries can claim lives and destroy hundreds of thousands of forest acreage and millions of dollars worth of homes. One of the biggest fires in Colorado's history was started by some goofy female ranger who decided to burn a letter. Once aflame, that little letter got away from her and ravaged everything in its path.

This is true of sex too. In the right context, sex is a good thing, a beautiful thing. It's a gift from our Lord. Outside of that context, however, it is incredibly destructive. It will destroy your life by making you its slave. Like the fire sparked by that single letter, sex will consume every-thing in your life.

Sex outside of marriage is not fulfilling. It's crazy-making. It's like you've contracted poison ivy and you know it's completely irrational and illogical to keep scratching—because scratching won't make it go away—but you can't seem to stop. You give in to the urge and scratch that itch, get a brief—*brief*—bit of gratification, and then the itch spreads and the urge to scratch increases. Horrible, isn't it? It's just like sin. I think that may be why poison ivy exists, so that we could get a

good picture of the nature of sin. The man who goes about his life trying to find happiness through sex is going to be one itchy man—tormented by an urge that will never diminish but only continue to grow.

This same warning applies to romantic affection. If not kept in the proper context, romantic affection has the power to ruin you. Outside the boundaries established by God, it's absolutely destructive.

It may sound terribly old-fashioned, but I suggest to you that it is a sin to enter into a romantic relationship for no reason except the gratifi-cation of some emotional need. A relationship established with that motive is just plain wrong. Are you familiar with Romans 14:23, which states that "*whatsoever is not of faith is sin?*" If you don't know that verse already, you should familiarize yourself with it. Write it down. Applied to this subject, what it means is that if you cannot say that the thing you're doing—let's say the relationship you're involved in—is something you know the Lord Jesus wants you doing, then it's sin. You're outside of God's will. If it's not of faith, it is sin—no matter how old you are. If you're in a relationship just to gratify your flesh, you're sinning.

Young kids are very susceptible to this trap. It's acceptable, and even expected, that thirteen- and fourteen-year-old kids will have a boyfriend or girlfriend. Everyone is looking to "go steady," although in reality, you're not going anywhere at all. You're too young. You're years away from any serious consideration of marriage, so everything between now and then is just a game.

Can I make an observation here? I'd like to point out to you that the Scriptures do not acknowledge the existence of what we call, in our culture, "boyfriends and girlfriends." To the eyes of our Lord, a person is either single or married. There is nothing in between those two, except for a brief time of engagement. Our sinful culture has created a level of commitment that is something more than brotherly and yet something much less than marriage. And it's dangerous. It presumes the right to engage in physical expressions of affection that in truth, only belong to the married. To be blunt, those physical expressions are ultimately a form of foreplay. Consider the analogy of a kid not yet licensed to drive a car who sits behind the wheel with the engine running. Though he has no intention of taking the car anywhere, he revs the engine with one hand on the shifting lever and his foot on the gas peddle. It's foolishness for him to even be there, just one click of the transmission away from breaking the law.

It is a big mistake to fuel romantic feelings that are not going to go anywhere. I discourage that with all of my heart.

How do fires get ignited? They ignite by the sparks that fly when two people make eye contact or say just the right words to one another. Those sparks start a little fire, but in order to make it grow, you have to add fuel. Love letters, whispered words, body language—all those actions add kindling to the fire. Unless you're planning to marry that person, you're playing with fire—and setting yourself up for a severe burn.

Now, am I saying that you should not even consider romantic feelings with anybody unless you're planning to marry that person? Yep. That's exactly what I'm suggesting. You make a mistake going from romance to romance. Sooner or later, each of those relationships will end, and usually with someone getting burned in the process. But that's not how we do things as Christians. The Lord Jesus has a better way.

Just as emotions can be fueled, they can also be quenched. Misplaced affections can be killed. If you've allowed something to be sparked and fueled that you *know* is not God's will for you, you need to kill that thing. You need to cut it off before it can spread out of control. How you do that is by starving it of fuel. You quit saying the words and stop giving the looks that ignited the romance in the first place.

If you're serious about guarding your heart and protecting your emotions, you need to get a good grasp of the armor of God as described in Ephesians chapter six. You need to understand why you've been given a shield of faith, and what it's able to do. The Word tells us that we're to "*take up the shield of faith, with which you can extinguish all the flaming arrows of the evil one*" (Ephesians 6:16 NIV). Think about it. Satan is shooting fire at you. Why fiery darts? Because he wants to ignite something in you. Every temptation comes in the form of some kind of passion, lust, or desire—which has the potential to start a fire. But the shield of faith has the capacity to not just deflect the fiery darts, but also to quench the fire entirely.

I suggest to you that living by faith is living by what you know to be the truth and holding fast to it. It's not following emotion, but following the King and quenching every misplaced emotion. It's incredibly easy to fall in love. In fact, it's easier to fall in love than it is to stay in love. Falling in it is as easy as catching your clothes on fire. Don't let it happen. You *are* in control. Guard your heart and hold on.

Your mate is out there somewhere.

.

CHAPTER **9**

HCLD ON

"wait on the LORD; be of good courage,
and He shall strengthen your heart;
wait, I say, on the LORD."

psalm 27:14 (NKJV)

There's a very real possibility that you've already met the person you're going to marry. It may be that you've known the person for a while and you're just unaware that he or she is the one. You're oblivious. Or, it may be that there's someone in your life that you've been taking second and third looks at lately. You have a suspicion, or a sense, that this may very well be the person the Lord Jesus has brought to be your life partner. Perhaps you're already praying about that hope. Keep praying. Just make sure those prayers

don't include a lot of phrases like, "My will be done, Lord," or "C'mon, God—make 'em love me," or "Do this one thing for me and I'll serve You forever." If there's a person in your life that looks like "The One," lift them up in prayer and ask your Lord to have His perfect way with both your lives. And mean it.

Regardless of whether or not you already have your eye on "The One," God does. God sees that person. He's up high enough that He sees it all. He knows the name of your mate, He sees where that person is, and He knows everything that they're going through. He knows the number of hairs on their head, He knows all the things that they're thinking, all the experiences of life that they're going through, and He knows the work He's doing in that person before He brings the two of you together.

I maintain a strong conviction that every single person ought to live their life as though they were already committed to a life partner— because you are. Just because you don't clearly see yet who that person is doesn't mean they don't exist. They're out there somewhere.

This is why it's so important that you don't run around jumping into relationships and expressing all those romantic affections for someone when you don't have a clear conviction that he or she is the person the Lord Jesus created for you. Even if you don't know who you're being unfaithful to, you're still being unfaithful.

Does that sound weird to you? If it does, it's because you're worldly. What I'm telling you is just the commonsense truth. If your Father has called you to marriage, then you already belong to someone. You need to act like it. You need to begin to be faithful to the real, live person you will someday see face-to-face. If you don't, you're going to leave a long string of regrets behind you—reference points you wish you didn't have, memories you wish you could forget. Too many people carry that kind of baggage into their marriage. They bring in the residue of a long line of romances that burned real hot and then burned out. I don't want that for you. I want you to be able to give yourself passionately to one person and do so without the burden of regret.

So, how do you live as though your heart already belongs to someone? How do you live a faithful life to the one who hasn't yet been revealed to you? Simple. Here are four things you need to do:

Treat every person you meet as the brother or the sister that they are. Until the Lord Jesus says otherwise, everyone in your life is either a brother or a sister. They're a sibling. Write that down: "Everyone is my sibling, until God says something different." That's what the people in your life are and what they should remain—brothers and sisters. With that in mind:

Refrain from any and all romantic expressions of affection. If you're promised to an unknown mate, you need to keep your emotions in check. Don't do anything that would fuel a romance. No enticing looks or intriguing words or flirtatious behavior of any kind. These are your brothers and sisters, remember?

Pray God's will for everyone you meet. You can't go wrong doing this. And you wouldn't want it any other way. You want God's perfect will to be lived out in your life, in the life of your future mate, and in the lives of your brothers and sisters. Praying God's will reminds you to not try to seek your own.

Be busy about your Father's business. There's kingdom work to be done. Keep yourself occupied with whatever work God would have you do and wait for Him to bring your mate to you.

My daughter recently said, after hearing me encouraging someone on that last point, "You make it sound like that person is just going to magically appear, like if you just keep busy, then, bam!—that person is just going to show up and you're going to know it instantly."

I don't think that's the case. I'm not making that promise. But I do believe we're back to the "watched pot" scenario. Why stand staring down the street for your mate to appear when you could be occupying your time doing worthwhile work for the kingdom?

Commit yourself to your life partner. See yourself as belonging to that person already. Be faithful. Be busy. Be in group fellowship. Be in prayer. And one day, probably when you least expect it, the Lord Jesus is going to tap you on your shoulder and introduce you to the person He's brought to be your life mate. He'll give you the green light.

"And then?" you ask.

I have some suggestions about that as well.

CHAPTER **10**

GO

"therefore let us not judge one another
anymore, but rather resolve this,
not to put a stumbling block
or a cause to fall
in our brother's way."

romans 14:13 (NKJV)

IT'S NOT NECESSARY TO GET ALONE IN A CAR TO GET ACQUAINTED.

When you get a green light, you go . . . right?

Well, yes and no. You go, but you go with caution. When it comes to this one most important human-to-human relationship, the one you've been waiting for and hoping for and dreaming of, you proceed ahead when the Lord Jesus gives you the green light . . . but you do so carefully.

Here's an ideal scenario: You've been faithfully living your life as the promised partner to an unknown mate. You've been busy. You've occupied yourself with kingdom work and immersed yourself in the things of God. Some of that has included fellowship with the brothers and sisters in your church. After a time, someone in that group of siblings began to stand out to you. A suspicion grew, and you brought your questions to the Lord Jesus in prayer. The more you prayed, the more you began to sense that He was saying "yes" to this one person. If you're a man, the light finally dawned on you that you had *found* the woman! If you're a woman, you realized that you had *found* the man!

And then you threw off all restraint, spent all kinds of time alone, and let the passion pour, right?

Wrong. That's exactly wrong. Just because you finally get the green light from the Lord Jesus doesn't mean He wants you to start pretending the two of you are already life partners. That green light doesn't give you the go-ahead to start seeking out dark corners and getting alone by candlelight and getting busy getting affectionate. What you really need to do is just continue in that relationship as a sister, as a brother, and watch and see what the Lord Jesus does. You wait. Eventually, God will let you get more hokey and go all Romeo on the object of your affection, but you do nothing that is what I would call romantic until you've got a clear direction from Him that you should move in that direction.

The same danger that we discussed in chapter eight still exists in chapter ten. Sex still has the power to destroy your life. The same traps and snares lie along the path. Long, lingering looks still have the capacity to start a fire. So you avoid those stupid little games and treat each other with respect.

You may ask, "Well, how are we supposed to get to know each other then?" Not by candlelight. It's not necessary to get alone in a car to get acquainted. I discourage that with all of my heart. I think it's a mistake to try to draw each other away secretly. Not only is it a mistake, but it's also inconsiderate because it shows a complete lack of concern for the other person's reputation. It's also more than a little prideful. You may think you can stand firm, but when we think that, we have a tendency to fall.

Listen to me—the process of discovery must be pure. It does not involve test-driving lips or any other body parts, for that matter. In the context of keeping your relationship brotherly and sisterly until marriage—or at least until engagement—may I suggest that a lip kiss is not for siblings? A kiss on the lips is a sexual act. It is not the will of our Lord and Maker that we should know such intimate things as the taste of someone's lips or the smell of their hair unless that person is our life partner.

Stay in the company of your brothers and sisters. Get to know one another in the safety of that group, where you'll be sure to keep it on the brother-sister level. Remember the words of the Lord Jesus in Matthew 10:16 when He said, "*Therefore, be wise as serpents and innocent as doves*" (NIV). The King James Version uses the phrase "*harmless as doves.*" That ought to be you—harmless. You don't want to hurt anybody, do you? You don't want to cause anyone to stumble. There's probably no more dangerous period than when you've found the person you're going to spend the rest of your life with, but you aren't yet married. Once you're at this place of discovery and realization, you're very, very vulnerable. This is the point at which many people do foolish things.

To avoid all that, I encourage you to follow these guidelines:

Limit yourself. Listen to me—you've got to hold yourself back and limit those expressions of affection. Every single adult male knows there's a stupid high school boy living inside who is dying to come out and say all kinds of really idiotic things you can't ever back up. Hold your tongue, brother. Restrain yourself. Once you have chosen that person and you say, "This is it," (and by the way, that person has to agree) then this is now the time for you to be the leader. Draw some lines. Determine how far you're going to go in showing affection to that sister.

Consider the other. The Lord Jesus warned us, in Matthew 18:7, that "*Temptation to do wrong is inevitable, but how terrible it will be for* *the person who does the tempting*" (NLT). Do you want to be the tempter? Do you want to be the one who is causing your sister in the Lord, your brother in the Lord, to want to sin? To do so would be putting your relationship with your Lord in a major strain. You don't want to do that. Like Paul, who determined in 1 Corinthians that he wouldn't do anything—eat meat, drink wine, anything—that would cause another to stumble, determine that you will not become a temptation to the other person. You will not be responsible for them falling.

Be an example. People are watching you. They want to see how you're going to handle this relationship. Factor that into all your decisions. It's not the two of you on an island—other people are involved in your lives and watching your behavior. Don't blow your whole witness by having other people see you coming in and out of each other's apartments at all hours of the night. On that note, as Christian men and women, let me say that I see no reason why the two of you should be alone in an apartment *ever* prior to your marriage. Take heed lest you fall. Realize the power of human passion, and keep in mind that things happen in enclosed spaces that would never happen on the street.

Be accountable. Let me ask you this: are you a fiercely independent person, or are you wise enough to seek godly counsel and become accountable to another person? Obviously, from the way I've worded my question, I think the only wise recourse is to make yourself accountable to another. The Lord Jesus establishes authority figures in our lives to provide safety and guidance. Are you wise enough to accept that counsel from your parents, your pastor, your older brothers and sisters in the Lord?

Let me prove to you how seriously I take my role as spiritual counselor and older brother in the Lord.

A friend of mine, who I've worked with in the music ministry, was living a few hours from our church when he met the girl he was to marry. She attended our church and he had been commuting from that distance to serve in the music ministry here.

One night, I called his house and found out that she was there with him . . . a few hours away . . . at nighttime. I flipped my lid.

He answered by saying, "C'mon, man, we're Christians—we're not going to do anything." And he gave me this little speech about how fine they were with it and how I shouldn't worry.

I gave a little speech of my own, using some strong threats. I said, "You either find another arrangement tonight, or you ain't playing any more music with me." I told him that was how serious I was about wanting the best for the two of them. And you know what? Later on—not that night, but later on—he thanked me. They're married today and God is blessing both their marriage and their ministry. I think it's because they were accountable.

That's not the only time I've used strong words to pull a friend out of a dangerous situation. After discovering that another friend was at his girlfriend's apartment one night, I called, asked to speak to him, and told him to get out of there *now*. I have no problem doing that, because in so doing, I believe I've kept some brothers out of trouble. When you love someone, you look out for them.

We have to do that for one another. It only works if you're of one mind and you both understand the intent behind the rebuke. If you're in a relationship that is headed toward marriage, I urge you to submit yourself to those who love you enough to confront and correct you when you head in a wrong direction. Don't try to go it alone. Don't fool yourself into thinking you can just follow your own heart, your own instincts. Be wise—put yourself under that kind of accountability.

My prayer for you, as I've written this book, is that you will walk this journey in the order I've listed: that you will first know your Master, and begin to understand how great and wide and deep is His love for you; that you will realize your purpose and your mission, and gain an understanding of how a life partner fits into that; and that finally—then and only then—you will meet the one the Lord Jesus has intended for you since before you first drew breath.

Godspeed on your journey. May your life be long, rich, and meaningful.

Father, I ask the best for my brothers and my sisters. I ask that You'll take the truths that have been explained here from Your Word and You will use them to guide and minister to the brother, the sister, who is reading this now. Make Your character and Your will known, Father. Be glorified in this life.

ABOUT THE AUTHOR

On the same day God grabbed hold of thirteen-year-old Ken Graves, He also put a call on his life. Ken understood that he was to go into the ministry. As he says, he "knew from that moment on that life was about one thing: the Lord Jesus."

With his focus directly on Jesus, Ken dropped out of school at sixteen and sent himself to "Gospel boot camp"—an Alabama work farm intended to rehabilitate outlaws. For Ken, it was a chance to immerse himself in God's Word. He spent four years there learning from his spiritual advisors and ministering as a staff member.

Though Ken had intended to do otherwise, God eventually called him back to the woods of his home state, Maine. As he and his wife, Jeanette, began their life together, Ken first supported them from the end of a chainsaw, where he began to collect scar tissue. On the side, he hooked up with a band and started ministering through music. It wasn't long, though, before he began preaching and teaching. In 1986, Calvary Chapel Bangor was born.

When he's not ministering to his church family, Ken spends his days thinking about God, walking the woods, or paddling about on his sea kayak. As he says, "I'm just up here in my little corner trying to do the thing the Lord Jesus has told me to do."

BIBLE STUDY GUIDE

Want to go deeper? Grab your Bible and a pen—and see what God's Word has to say to you on the subject of your Master, your mission, and your mate.

CHAPTER ONE

1. Is the notion of God not only creating, but approving of romance, a new idea for you?

2. Read John 15:13 and Romans 5:8. What is our Father's definition of love?

3. How does the world define love?

4. Why is the world's love so fleeting?

CHAPTER TWO

1. Read Romans 12:2 (NLT) again: *"Don't copy the behavior and customs of this world, but let God transform you into a new person by changing the way you think. Then you will know what God wants you to do, and you will know how good and pleasing and perfect his will really is."* It is clear that God is willing to change you into a new person. What stands in the way of transformation?

   a. What brings about transformation?

2. Having grown up in this world, you no doubt have adopted some *"behavior and customs of this world."* Take a moment to think about your mindset toward love, romance, and the seeking of a mate. In which areas do you need to change, and how?

   a. My attitudes/beliefs_____
   _____

   b. My actions/behavior_____
   _____

   c. My expectations_____
   _____

3. Some people fear that if they surrender their lives to God, He will turn them in a direction they don't want to go. What are your thoughts about submitting to the will of God?

a. How does Romans 12:2 describe God's will?

4. What is your motive for marriage?

CHAPTER THREE

1. Let's look at Psalm 139 in four parts:

   a. Verses 1–6: What does God know about you?

   b. Verses 7–12: Where is God in relation to you?

   c. Verses 13–18: Who decided the color of your hair, skin, and eyes . . . your fingerprints . . . your height . . . your gender?

      (1.) Before you lived a single day, what did God do? (Verse 16)

   d. Verses 19–24: Write verse 23 here.

      (1.) What anxieties do you need to express to the Lord?

2. Considering everything Psalm 139 proclaims, write what you believe about God's plan for your life.

3. Has the Lord spoken to you about your mission? If so, what is He calling you to do?

4. Read Isaiah 30:21 and write it here.

   a. What confidence does this give you concerning your mission and your mate?

Chapter Four

1. Read the following verses and write down who is receiving attention, protection, and guidance from the Lord:
   a. Leviticus 19:10

   b. Psalm 68:6

   c. Psalm 146:7–9

2. How would you answer someone who claimed that God is an absent, detached, "hands-off" Creator?

3. Read Proverbs 3:5–6. What does the Lord desire for you to do?

    a. What will He do in return?

4. Read Romans 5:8–10. What were you when the Lord Jesus died for you? (Verse 8)

    a. What were you when God reconciled you to Himself? (Verse 10)

    b. If the Lord Jesus died for you and reconciled you to Himself when you were estranged from Him, is it reasonable to worry now—as His beloved—that you could possibly lose His love and affection?

CHAPTER FIVE

1. Read Ephesians 2:10. According to this verse, when was your particular life mission chosen for you?

2. Read the following verses and list whether that verse portrays God's "lamb" side or His "lion" side:
   a. Psalm 145:8, 9

   b. Isaiah 53:6, 7

   c. Joel 3:16

   d. Revelation 19:11–16

3. What "lion" tendencies do men bring into marriage? What "lamb"
   characteristics do women provide? List the traits that would benefit
   a couple in fulfilling their life mission and in raising their children:

Lion	Lamb

5. Think about your particular mission—that unique work that your
   Father has created you to do. How might a spouse help you fulfill that specific task better than you could alone?

CHAPTER SIX

1. In this chapter, Pastor Ken stated that if your relationship with Jesus is brand new, you should wait before beginning to consider a mate. Take stock of your walk: How long has Jesus been not just your Savior, but your Lord?

2. In 2 Corinthians 6:14, God warns us, "*Do not be yoked together with unbelievers. For what do righteousness and wickedness have in common? Or what fellowship can light have with darkness?*" (NIV). No doubt, you've known unbelievers that you have much in common with: work, hobbies, likes, and dislikes. If this verse is not addressing those types of shared interests, what do you think it's referring to?

3. Men: Read Proverbs 31:10–31. In your opinion, could a woman attain this kind of character on sheer determination alone? If not, what does it take to turn a sinful, selfish human being into a model of virtue?

   Women: Read 1 Timothy 3:1–13. Which of these qualities do you *not* want in a man who will lead your home—a man that you, as a woman of God, will submit to?

4. Do you understand the blessing that comes from waiting for a Jesus man or a Jesus woman? Write a statement of commitment—a promise to yourself that you will not compromise or settle for less than God's best for you.

CHAPTER SEVEN

1. Read Genesis 24:3b, 4. Rewrite this verse as though the Lord is instructing the Holy Spirit on where to find your mate. Personalize this statement, using your own name.

2. It is easy to worry that God is not as concerned with your need for a spouse as you are. But that's a needless worry. Read Matthew 6:8 and rewrite this verse to address your need of a mate.

3. What comfort do you find from Luke 12:29–32?

4. Where, specifically, might you busy yourself doing kingdom work? Make a list of need areas within your church or your community where you can be used by your Father to make a difference.

CHAPTER EIGHT

1. Pastor Ken wrote, *"While you're waiting for the Lord Jesus to bring a mate to you, your job is to guard your heart."* How have you done in that regard prior to now?

2. Read Matthew 6:21. Be completely honest: where is your heart today?

3. Read Colossians 3:2. What changes can you make in order to fulfill this verse?

4. In this chapter, we were encouraged to *"quench every misplaced emotion."* According to Galatians 5:16, how can we do this?

CHAPTER NINE

1. We sometimes direct God too specifically in our prayers. "Here's what I want, Lord, and here's how You can get it for me." According to Matthew 6:10, how should we pray?

2. From what you learn in Proverbs 19:21, why is it wise to pray for your Father's will to be done, rather than your own?

3. Though it might feel like a strain on your heart to have to hold back and wait for God's timing, what really happens when you wait on the Lord, according to Psalm 27:14?

4. Write a prayer asking God to protect and strengthen your unknown mate.

Chapter Ten

1. Read 1 Corinthians 10:12. What caution is the Lord speaking to you through this verse?

2. First Thessalonians 5:22 warns us to "*Abstain from all appearance of evil.*" How might you being in the "wrong place at the wrong time" (an appearance of evil) stumble another brother or sister?

3. Read James 1:13–16. How can 2 Corinthians 10:3–5 (particularly 5b) help you stop the progression from desire to sin to death?

4. Are there people watching over your soul? Read Hebrews 13:17 and make a list of those God has placed in authority over you. Then—commit to submit.